Origins

Shiver me Timbers!

Chris Powling ■ Jonatronix

OXFORD
UNIVERSITY PRESS

In this story ...

Mrs Mills

Long John Lucy

Max

Ant

Tiger

Cat

3

Chapter 1 – The Pirate Fair

"Welcome aboard, me hearties," beamed Mrs Mills, the head teacher. "We need all the treasure you can find for our new school bus. Yo-ho-ho!"

"Yo-ho-ho?" said Cat. "She means yo-ho-hopeless, doesn't she? A school bus will cost loads of money."

"This is just a start, Cat," Max told her.

"Anyway," Tiger grinned, "a pirate fair is much more fun than our normal summer fair. We may even win a prize."

"I'd love to win the best-dressed pirate contest!" said Cat.

"Me too," said Ant. "But it won't be easy. I can see pirate costumes everywhere."

"Yes, and all of them are rubbish," came a familiar voice. "The best-dressed pirate is standing right behind you!"

Cat, Ant and Tiger groaned out loud. Even Max pulled a face.

"Lucy!" he said.

"That's Long John Lucy to you," Lucy sniffed. "I'm the prettiest pirate here."

"Pirates aren't pretty!" snorted Tiger.

"This one is," said Lucy.

Lucy shook her golden curls. She was a terrible show off, but even Tiger had to agree – she was the best-dressed pirate at the fair. Lucy's pirate costume was perfect. No coat had ever looked so crimson. No hat had ever looked so black. Even her wooden leg looked real.

Lucy was bound to win a prize.

Chapter 2 – Ship ahoy!

To cheer themselves up, the children went to see if they could win a different prize. Lucy followed them.

At the Hook a Ship stall there was a pirate pool. Lots of model pirate ships bib-bobbed on the water, smart as new paint.

Lucky Sand Pit Treasure Dip

"Ahoy there, shipmates!" said the lady by the stall. "Would you like a go?"

"Yes please!" cried the children.

"I'm first," said Lucy, pushing in.

on the Parrot

"Just hook a ship to win," said the lady, handing Lucy a fishing rod.

"Easy-peasy," said Lucy.

"Let's make it not so easy," whispered Max.

Max, Cat, Ant and Tiger crept behind the stall. They turned the dials on their watches and …

The four micro-friends climbed up a hose at the side of the pirate pool. Luckily, one of the ships was close to the edge.

"All aboard!" cried Captain Max.

The children clambered down on to the deck of the model ship. It bibbed and bobbed beneath them. Max steered the ship away from the side.

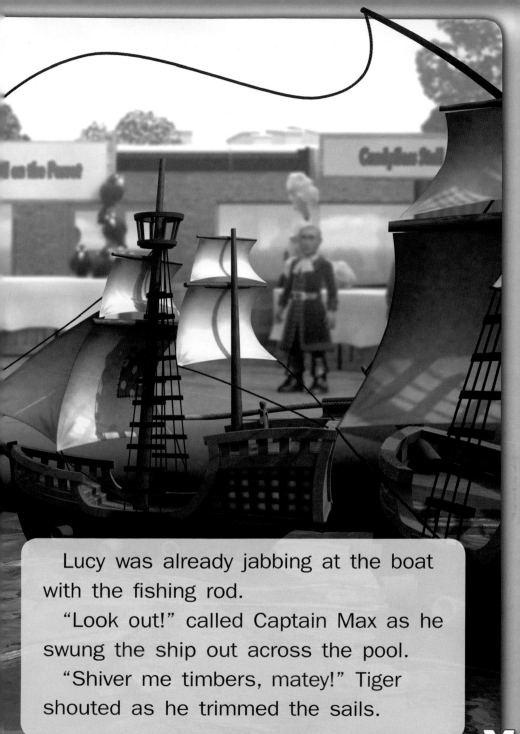

Lucy was already jabbing at the boat with the fishing rod.

"Look out!" called Captain Max as he swung the ship out across the pool.

"Shiver me timbers, matey!" Tiger shouted as he trimmed the sails.

"She's coming!" cried Ant. "Hard to starboard."

"Which way is that?" asked Max.

"Right!" called out Cat.

Max spun the ship's wheel and the pirate ship swung to the right. Soon they were tacking across the paddling pool, dodging the fish hook.

Lucy kept dipping her fishing rod into the water but she missed the ship every time. At first she was baffled. Then she got cross. Finally, she lost her temper.

"Take *that* you stupid boat!" she screamed at the top of her voice.

This time, she really did shiver its timbers.

Water splashed on to the deck.
The ship rocked and rolled.

"She's trying to sink us!" cried Cat.

"Hold on tight!" shouted Max.

Ant grabbed on to the rigging. Cat clung
to the mast.

The ship heaved up and down in the water. Max did his best to steer.

"I can't hold on much longer!" cried Ant.

"I don't feel well," groaned Tiger.

Then Cat had an idea ...

Mrs Mills got up on the stage. "Now for the winners of the best-dressed pirate contest," she announced. "It's Max, Cat, Ant and Tiger!"

"Us?" they gasped.

"Them?" squealed Long John Lucy.

"Yes," said Mrs Mills. "Real pirates weren't neat and tidy, you know. They were as wet and dirty as you are!"

Everyone burst out clapping.

Well, almost everyone … the pirate with the crimson coat, the black hat and the wooden leg was too busy having a tantrum.

School Fair

Candyfloss Stall

Find out more ...

Ever wondered what real pirates did, what they ate, or how they boarded an enemy ship? Find all the answers and more in *Pirates.*

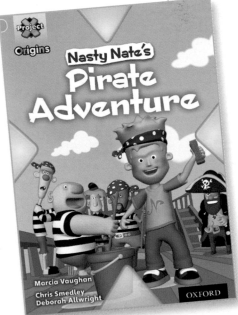

For more pirate fun read *Nasty Nate's Pirate Adventure*.